BREAKING NEW GROUNDS

UNLOCKING REALMS AND CONNECTIONS THROUGH KINGDOM KEYS

DR. MITCHELL FOSTER

ISBN: 979-8-9901302-5-8

"The key of the house of David I will lay on his shoulder;
so he shall open, and no one shall shut;
and he shall shut, and no one shall open."
Isaiah 22:22 (NKJV)

FOREWORD

There are books that inform, and there are books that unlock. *Breaking New Grounds; Unlocking Realms And Connections Through Kingdom Keys* carries the kind of revelation that does both.

Dr. Mitchell Foster has written a work that speaks directly to a people in transition, to builders in motion, to pioneers under pressure, and to believers who know they are standing at the edge of something greater but need the wisdom of God to move rightly. This book is not casual revelation. It is a summons to discernment, stewardship, and Kingdom movement.

The subject of keys is not minor in scripture, and it is not minor in this hour. Keys represent access, authority, responsibility, and governmental permission. They speak to what can be opened, what must remain shut, what must be guarded, and what must be stewarded with maturity. Far too many want doors without discipline, access without alignment, and influence without weight-bearing capacity. But God does not release greater realms to the careless. God funds what He can trust. Stewardship precedes increase.

What Dr. Foster does well in this book is bring the reader beyond inspiration and into responsibility. He shows that breaking new ground is not merely about desire, ambition, or even prophetic excitement. It is about understanding the right key, the right door, the right timing, the right relationships, and the right posture before God. That is where many miss it. They are reaching for open doors while ignoring the formation required to sustain what those doors will demand.

This message is timely because many are in a season where the Lord is shifting their language, stretching their faith, refining their connections, and repositioning their assignments. You are not behind, you are being positioned. But divine positioning must be met with divine understanding. Alignment over attention. Noise has never built anything in the Kingdom. Structure does. Obedience does. Wisdom does.

As I read the framework of this book, I could see that Dr. Foster is not just trying to inspire readers to think about keys symbolically. He is pressing the issue of how believers must handle revelation in practical, weighty, and accountable ways. He deals with authority, access, destiny connections, timing, prosperity, and the power of the right questions. That is a needed progression because keys are never just about entry. They are also about administration. Once a door opens, can you govern what is on the other side with wisdom? Can you carry what you prayed for? Can you protect what God entrusted to you? Can you discern when a connection is covenant and when it is only convenient?

These are not shallow matters. These are the kinds of realities that separate sincere believers from mature builders.

I also appreciate that this book does not romanticize breakthrough. It gives language to process. It helps the reader understand that spiritual access comes with holy weight. In every season, God is looking for those who will not mishandle revelation, misuse authority, or misinterpret movement. He is looking for those who understand that obedience with wisdom is better than speed without discernment.

Dr. Mitchell Foster writes with conviction and with the heart of one who understands that revelation must produce fruit. His burden is evident. His intent is clear. He wants the people of God to recognize what Heaven has placed within their reach and to move in a way that honors both the power and the responsibility of that access.

This book will challenge leaders, prophetic people, intercessors, pioneers, and emerging builders to examine how they are handling the keys in their lives. It will call some into deeper consecration. It will call others into sharper strategy. It will call many to repent for treating sacred access lightly. And for those who are ready, it will provide language and framework for the next stage of their Kingdom assignment.

This is not the hour for vague revelation and undisciplined movement. This is the hour for consecrated access, disciplined stewardship, and obedience with wisdom. There is ground to take, doors to unlock, and assignments to fulfill, but none of it will be sustained without alignment. The Lord is still granting keys, but He is placing them on the shoulders of those who understand weight, not just wonder.

Receive this book prayerfully. Read it with humility. Walk through it with maturity. And let the Spirit of the Lord expose every place in your life where you have desired access without preparation, authority without submission, or breakthrough without structure. Then let Him bring you into Goshen, into the place of divine preservation, provision, and clarity, where what He has ordained for your life can be built well and stewarded rightly.

May this book unlock revelation. May it strengthen your discernment. May it refine your stewardship. And may it position you to carry, with integrity and power, every Kingdom key God has entrusted to your hands.

Dwann K. Holmes

Founder, The Global Institute of Church & Marketplace Prophets

TABLE OF CONTENTS

INTRODUCTION

The Prophetic Grace of Spiritual Keys

Zechariah 4:6-7 (NKJV): "So he answered and said to me: 'This is the word of the Lord to Zerubbabel: 'Not by might nor by power, but by My Spirit,' says the Lord of hosts. 'Who are you, O great mountain? Before Zerubbabel, you shall become a plain! And he shall bring forth the capstone with shouts of "Grace, grace to it!"'

Keys are prophetic symbols that appear eight times in the Bible. Six of the verses are found in the New Testament and two verses are in the Old Testament. Isaiah 22:22 and Matthew 16:19 are two of the most prayed and prophesied verses when it comes to keys and access.

One verse mentions open doors that no man can open or shut, while the other proclaims a governing capability to legislate what can be loosed or bound. One gives access while the other releases deliverance. Both operate in power and authority.

But there is one thing for certain: keys are more than prophetic symbols; they are spiritual tools that can unlock miracles, healing, deliverance, and breakthrough. They contain kingdom principles for advancement, engagement, dominion, and freedom.

There is such a prophetic grace that comes through spiritual keys: a grace that can conquer mountains, a grace that can only move by the Spirit of the Lord.

I experienced this grace in 2025 while serving on an apostolic assignment in Zimbabwe. Through the power of visions and one prophetic act, the Lord downloaded so much revelation that I am releasing to you as kingdom principles in this book.

BREAKING NEW GROUNDS: Unlocking Realms and Connections Through Kingdom Keys is a book that introduces five biblically based principles to expand your knowledge. My hope is that it will challenge you to find innovative ways to carry out the work of the kingdom and trust God in the midst of your journey. To break new ground is to follow God in obedience to the visions He has shown you and the instructions He has given you. It is the willingness to enter territories with a word to revive and a key to set free.

This book is organized in the following manner:

Each chapter begins with a foundational scripture that serves as the cornerstone for building upon the concept discussed.

Prophetic forecasts unlock the concept by giving a preview that introduces what it is and sets the tone for the impartation released through prophetic revelations and applications.

Keynote connections present biblical figures who illustrate the principles of the concept and additional spiritual keys that can be used.

Chapter forward summaries give a brief recap and prepare the reader for what's taking place in the next chapter.

BREAKING NEW GROUNDS: Unlocking Realms and Connections Through Kingdom Keys is for the apostolic and prophetic voices who are pioneering kingdom initiatives in new and familiar territories. It is for those who mentor and serve as a key to unlock the destinies of their mentees and spiritual children. Each chapter contains a wealth of information that invite strategic conversations on how to steward and execute God's plans. Let's begin by learning the art of breaking new ground through prophetic revelation.

CHAPTER 1

Breaking New Ground through Prophetic Revelation

Jeremiah 1:11 (NKJV): "Moreover the word of the Lord came to me, saying, 'Jeremiah, what do you see?'"

Prophetic Forecast: Unlocking the Concept

Apostles are the pioneers and forerunners who receive visions that are future forward and often do not make sense in the current time. These visions are downloaded from the mind of God. They are thoughts of innovation designed to bring kingdom solutions, technologies, and paradigms into nations, mountains of influence, and realms. This type of innovation needs a willing vessel who can be trusted to carry it to its full manifestation. Apostles are the visionaries whom God has graced to build systems and structures to house the creative technology of the vision.

Apostolic vision is what God's divine design looks like. Apostolic intelligence is God's strategy for building it.

Apostolic vision is a seed that contains everything within it to build with precision and ensure it stands up to the kingdom standard or code. It is the dominion mandate that brings forth fruit of its own kind and bears the spiritual DNA of the Creator (Genesis 1:11-12, 26-28). It requires a heart to obey, a voice to speak, a faith to activate, and an obedience to execute.

Stewarding this vision, often deemed unconventional, unorthodox, and let's face it, even downright crazy, is not for the faint of heart. In fact, it is for those who can see it completed in the spirit while waiting for it to unfold in the natural.

Apostles must be equipped with spiritual sight, insight, foresight, and fortitude. They must have the language to communicate what the natural mind does not have the ability to imagine. They also must accept that they only know in part, but God still expects full participation. Executing vision takes an apostolic grace to sustain the work and an anointing to finish despite opposition.

Breaking new ground is one of the apostle's major mantle distinctives, and this distinctive is key in disrupting systems with sound doctrine. It involves breaking through resistance while being diligent and resilient. Apostles remain focused on plowing and building with the ox anointing in whatever territory they have been sent. They also break new ground in mindsets by expanding revelation on kingdom principles.

Within the revelation lies deliverance.
Within the principle is a kingdom key of breakthrough.

Breaking new ground is not only about innovation, but it is also about access. We need a key to enter the door and walk through the gate of the territory. Our concept of keys can sometimes be limited to our natural or literal understanding. But the physical key that we see has a metaphorical meaning and a spiritual understanding. What's in the natural is temporary, and what's in the spirit is eternal and effective.

Keys are spiritual tools grounded in kingdom principles and protocol that do more than lock and unlock. They set free and set order, and they align what's misaligned. They connect and disconnect while authorizing permission to enter what's safeguarded. Keys are essential for movement, momentum, and the manifestation of God's word, plan, and will.

The vision is more than the blueprint.
It is the key to setting things in motion.

Prophetic Vision of the Keys

God has shown me many visions about keys. I have had visions where I saw tons of keys on a metal ring. I have also seen two keys: one gold, the other silver, regular in appearance, but they were long like ancient keys. The gold and silver keys both had little keys tied onto them. They were almost like generational keys that could unlock many things such as wealth. For example, if I could unlock wealth in my life, then it would affect all my children. I could open the door to generational blessings.

The colors stood out the most to me, so I began to research their meanings. The gold key represented divine authority, access into different dimensions, spiritual unlocking, and supernatural breakthroughs. It also signified royalty, power, and status as seen in the crown and the scepter. The silver key represented revelation, spiritual access, and divine authority.

Here I was with this significant vision and its revelation, and I still had this question for God, “What does all this mean?”

Prophetic Act: The Right Key for the Right Miracle

In 2025, God began to deal with me about nations and the people being unlocked in each one. He instructed me to take about 1,000 keys to Zimbabwe. I had to pray over them and keep them soaked in anointed prayer oil.

I proceeded to do as the Lord had shared with me, but I still asked, ”God, where do I get all these keys from?”

I found myself at Lowe's. A gentleman who worked and did maintenance told me that he could get me as many keys as I wanted. Now I had all the

keys that I needed to pray over, but I didn't know exactly what God was going to do with them. He just told me to follow the instructions that He would tell me.

I put the keys in a big container, soaked them in oil, and prayed over them every single day. When I was ready to go, I had all this oil dripping off these keys, so I put them in Ziploc bags. Then I was on my way to The Release of Fresh Fire conference in Zimbabwe.

I arrived at the church on time, which was a good thing. I was scheduled to be the first speaker. When I walked into the service, every one of the pastors was present and accounted for. The fathers in the land who cared deeply for and ministered faithfully to their congregation stood in close proximity. I still was not quite sure what God's plan was, but I was in place and ready to follow His lead.

I began to teach, and then God led me to invite people to the altar. The crowd flooded this intimate place of worship. He instructed me to pass out the keys to all the fathers in the land, the apostles, prophets, bishops, and the lay people. As I placed the key in each person's hand, the power of God laid them out in the spirit. The key unlocked something for them based on their needs.

Testimonies of breakthrough began to come back even before I left. One bishop, who was one of the fathers in the land, said that after he had gotten a key, the door he had been praying for suddenly opened for him. There was a young lady who didn't have the money to continue building her house, and she also didn't have any means of transportation. She came back and said God sent her not only the money to finish her house, but she also was granted a new car.

Another young lady whose cancer had come back received the miracle of healing in her body. Testimonies also came in from Kenya as I gave keys to the people there. One guy's church was small, but it grew exponentially from Kenya to Botswana, its neighboring country.

Who would've thought that something so small could produce a powerful demonstration of God's glory?

Prophetic Revelation: Spiritual Keys Shift Your Faith

It was almost apostolic that God was unlocking what they needed. I saw such a supernatural move as we prayed for about a thousand people. The testimonies are still coming in. I didn't even know that many of the people were in poverty, but they received miracles of financial provision. All I had done was put the key in their hands, and the power of God was just phenomenal.

Obedience to God's instructions, moving in His timing, receiving the prophetic vision, and demonstrating the prophetic act were spiritual keys that shifted a people into a greater level of faith in God.

Keynote Connection: Joseph

Genesis 41:41-42 (NKJV): "And Pharaoh said to Joseph, 'See, I have set you over all the land of Egypt.' Then Pharaoh took his signet ring off his hand and put it on Joseph's hand; and he clothed him in garments of fine linen and put a gold chain around his neck."

Dreams, like visions, can serve as spiritual keys that unlock prophetic destiny. We see this in the life of Joseph. He had an apostolic oil on him. Many believed him to be an apostolic prophet. Even though he was taken into captivity after being betrayed and sold into slavery by his brothers, Joseph's favor was a spiritual key that caused him to be prosperous in every space he found himself in.

His integrity and gift of dream interpretation were spiritual keys that enabled him to ascend to a second-in-command leadership position in Pharoah's kingdom. When he adorned Joseph with gold, it symbolized the high value of a spiritual worth. Joseph's spiritual keys indeed made room for him and set him before kings. His keys of strategic planning and execution led him to secure a place called Goshen for his family, a generational move essential for legacy and positioning to be established and God's covenantal plan to be fulfilled.

As his story concluded with the great declaration that what his brothers meant for evil was used for good to save a people (Genesis 50:20), Joseph teaches us that perhaps forgiveness is one of the most important spiritual keys for us to possess.

Chapter Forward: Breaking New Ground with the Right Foundation

After developers or contractors have broken new ground, they begin construction by building the right foundation. This is what this first chapter has done. It introduced the concept of spiritual keys, shared the prophetic vision, act, and revelation behind the concept, and ended with a keynote connection on Joseph, an apostolic and prophetic type who exemplified the concept. In addition to breaking new ground in your perspective of keys, this chapter sets the tone for the upcoming exploration of the many ways these spiritual keys function in our lives and our destinies.

CHAPTER 2

Keys as Authority, Access, and Responsibility

Matthew 16:16-19 (NKJV): "Simon Peter answered and said, 'You are the Christ, the Son of the living God.' Jesus answered and said to him, 'Blessed are you, Simon Bar-Jonah, for flesh and blood has not revealed this to you, but My Father who is in heaven. And I also say to you that you are Peter, and on this rock, I will build My church, and the gates of Hades shall not prevail against it. And I will give you the keys of the kingdom of heaven, and whatever you bind on earth will be bound in heaven, and whatever you loose on earth will be loosed in heaven.'"

Prophetic Forecast: Unlocking the Concept

Spiritual keys represent authority, access, responsibility, and stewardship. As apostles, we train many people all over this world. In order for them to get the true insights, something must be unlocked in them.

We don't realize that there are people in our lives who are divinely assigned to get us to the next place.

Throughout Scripture, we see people unlock wealth and healing. Deliverance was unlocked so that people could get what they needed. Sometimes we don't understand that it is just a key. Also, we must truly understand that it is Jesus who holds these keys and gives us access.

He is the door, the way, the truth, and the life. He is the Master Unlocker. We are His vessels to help others receive the breakthrough they need, even if that breakthrough is exposing the lie, the error, and the faulty foundations through the Spirit of Truth.

The name and nature of Jesus are keys that unlock realms within us:

Phil.2:9-11; Isa.9:6-7; Prov.18:10
Matt.16:19; Matt.18:18-20; Rom.8:38-39; 1Cor.13:13

- *a key of salvation and deliverance; a key of healing and wholeness.*
- *a key of power and authority; a key of access and position.*
- *a key of posture and prayer; a key of humility and obedience.*
- *a key of joy and peace; a key of counsel and might.*
- *a key of wisdom, understanding, and knowledge.*
- *a key of love – the greatest force known to break the hardness of any ground, any heart, and any mind.*

That's why Jesus told Peter that He was giving him the keys in the opening scripture. As I meditated on these verses, I began to inquire of God. "Okay, God. What do You mean by that?"

He said, "I'm giving him the keys to be able to go into My church and unlock those things that really need to be unlocked for the advancement of My kingdom."

I finally understood that this scripture was more about ownership and stewardship of keys. The Lord kept emphasizing the authority and the responsibility of the keys. More importantly, I began to gain more insight into the power of access.

Ownership means that you hold possession of something. The deeds are in your name. No one else can claim that it belongs to them. A governmental entity has processed legal documentation that shows proof of ownership, and it maintains a copy kept on record.

This sounds like the Courts of Heaven, doesn't it?

The Word of God is our legal documentation and code by which we stand and present as our evidence. The Courts of Heaven house and legislate that word. We have grace to enter boldly to petition our case. The treasury of the Lord contains our deeds and our prophetic scrolls. We have to recognize the great treasure we have gained through our Lord and Savior, Jesus Christ. He has given us the keys of authority, access, and grace.

With that ownership comes the expectation to steward it well.

Stewardship is being entrusted to manage something that is owned, either by you or someone else. Managing it means making sure it is well taken of. For example, good stewardship of a house looks like keeping up with the repairs, renovating when needed, and maintaining the lawn.

The Lord entrusts us to be good stewards of His provision. He supplies our every need, gives us resources, and expects us to manage it with the key of wisdom. In Genesis 2:15, He placed Adam in the Garden of Eden to work it, to guard it, to steward it. He was the chief manager of the dimension that the Lord created in seven days. He entrusted Adam with the key of dominion.

With that key of dominion came the weight of responsibility. It encompassed authority and access. He only had to follow one instruction: don't eat from the tree of the knowledge of good and evil. He had authority over this dimension and open access except for one tree.

One conversation shifted everything for Adam and his wife, Eve. That one subtle suggestion resulted in Adam losing his key to dominion. The key of subtlety opened the door to separation from God. Adam allowed a squatter to steal his keys of authority and access. He didn't steward well what God entrusted him with.

This is why Jesus is referred to as the last Adam or the second Adam in the Gospels (Romans 5:12-21; 1 Corinthians 15:45-49). His obedience saved many from the spiritual death caused by the first Adam's disobedience. Jesus "disarmed principalities and powers, [and] made a public spectacle of them, triumphing over them in it" (Colossians 2:15), and He retrieved the keys of death, hell, and the grave. He restored dominion, power, and authority to us.

Every pattern has a type that replicates its unique structure.
Heaven is the pattern; earth is the type.
Both declare the glory of God and serve as witnesses.
Both work with the key of authority (binding and loosing.)

Prophetic Revelation: Our Words are Keys That Unlock Authority

God has given us authority, and the authority is what unlocks. When apostles speak, authority is released out of them. Every time Jesus spoke a word, that was a key of authority. When He said, "Your faith has made you whole," there was authority in those words to heal and deliver. The key of faith works with the key of authority. We must have faith in what we say and understand that we can decree a thing, and it shall be established.

Prophetic Application: Keys of Access Become Keys That Educate

Keys can unlock access into dimensions that we cannot enter. They can help us to awaken, activate, or develop what has been lying dormant within us. Apostolic and prophetic mentors often serve as keys for people who are just emerging fully into their offices or need to sharpen and expand different parts of their mantles. For example, there was a young lady who was a prophetess serving on my staff. I told her that she needed to connect with Apostle Dwann Holmes for training. She possessed the apostolic and prophetic keys that accessed a deeper level of the prophetic. She could challenge the young lady to stretch her capacity.

So what does that access look like on a mentorship level? It includes training people to understand how to discern the truth and how, when, and to whom to prophesy. It could be as simple as helping them answer the question, “Am I really a prophet?”

Mentors give insight to their mentees. Sometimes they don’t have insight of what a prophet should be or how to discern properly. So it is important that they go through this probation period of training. I believe that keys educate, and so when you educate, you unlock information or knowledge. Christ did it all the time.

Just by simply listening to their mentor, they will gain revelation that they would’ve never gotten if there was no connection. The unlocking is so impactful. The person would be like, “My God, where'd that come from?” They may also say, “I didn't know I had that.”

Having a teachable spirit and a heart of submission makes it so much easier to maximize the privilege of access.

Prophetic Accountability:

Are You Ready for the Weight of This Key?

Let's look at keys and responsibility using a natural example, my children. I'll say, "Listen, I'm going to allow you to use the keys to my car. But guess what? You're going to have to take a minute."

They have to go through that same probation period because access comes with responsibility. I look at keys also as ownership. My children will have to take some ownership in this. Because if I unlock something for you, then you've got to see it as yours, too.

Giving the keys to the car is like giving people access to my tribe. I'll say to that person, "Hey, I'm going to unlock this to you." I'm going to trust with them with the responsibility of whatever is being unlocked and hope that they will do what they said they were going to do. But sometimes that is not always the case. I've had people where I've put that responsibility in their hands and guess what? They've wrecked the car. So I would ask, "God, why did they wreck the car?"

God said, "Sometimes you would have never known that they were responsible if certain things wouldn't have happened."

And then the other side to that is you wanted that position filled quickly. So you unlocked something immature when they were not mature enough and ready to handle the responsibility.

When we traveled to Kenya, we had all these people telling us that they were ready to be affirmed. It was just a mess. One lady got mad at me and jumped off our platform because I told her that I would never affirm anybody. The people who were seeking affirmation didn't have anything. I could see no visible fruit of their mantles. They were not ready or prepared. I mean, some of them didn’t even know what an apostle was. They just wanted a name; the title meant more than the training and process.

People must demonstrate maturity and readiness before being entrusted with such authority given in spiritual keys. Put them on a probation period to see if they're going to be responsible. Eventually, you will find out if a person is serious or if they're not. Premature unlocking can lead to negative outcomes. As apostles, we must discern wisely who is ready to receive the key of responsibility.

Keynote Connection: Peter

1 Peter 4:10 (NKJV): "As each one has received a gift, minister it to one another, as good stewards of the manifold grace of God."

Let's go back to our opening scripture. Peter's story shows what the keys of authority, access, responsibility, and stewardship look like and how they function through a commission. Perhaps the ring that holds all these keys is God's manifold grace.

Through the help of the Holy Spirit, Peter discerned the identity of Jesus, and Jesus, functioning in His apostolic office, declared Peter's commission to build His house upon a rock, and the gates of hell would not prevail against it (Matthew 18:18).

Having an ear to hear what the Spirit was saying and having the boldness to speak it set Peter up to receive kingdom keys. Throughout the book of Acts, we read about how he stewarded these keys well and helped unlocked healing and deliverance as he shared the Gospel with the Jews first and then with the Gentiles through his encounter with Cornelius.

Peter's example shows us another set of keys. The key of divine design grounds us in our kingdom identity and purpose. We know who we are, whose we are, and what purpose for which God sent us into the earth. The key of spiritual hearing and the key of discernment help us to recognize the true meaning behind what is being said, asked, or done. Finally, the key of boldness in the Holy Spirit empowers us to contend for the faith and pursue our purpose, all-in and all dependent on God.

Chapter Forward: Breaking New Ground in the Right Position

This chapter explored the symbolism of keys in Peter's encounter with Jesus. Keys represent not only authority and access, but also responsibility and stewardship. They grant authority to unlock specific areas, such as healing, deliverance, and prosperity, and this authority must be handled responsibly. Keys can also be found in the name and nature of Jesus and Adam's experience of mishandling the keys of dominion and stewardship. Perhaps Adam illustrates why responsibility as a key is so important in the natural and the spiritual. Finally, the chapter examined keys of authority, access, and responsibility through our words and through mentorship and training. Keys of authority, access, responsibility, and stewardship are all about being in divine position and alignment. Now let's discuss keys and destiny connections.

CHAPTER 3

Keys and Destiny Connections

1 Kings 19:19-21 (NKJV): "So he departed from there, and found Elisha the son of Shaphat, who was plowing with twelve yoke of oxen before him, and he was with the twelfth. Then Elijah passed by him and threw his mantle on him. And he left the oxen and ran after Elijah, and said, 'Please let me kiss my father and my mother, and then I will follow you.' And he said to him, 'Go back again, for what have I done to you?' So Elisha turned back from him and took a yoke of oxen and slaughtered them and boiled their flesh, using the oxen's equipment, and gave it to the people, and they ate. Then he arose and followed Elijah and became his servant."

Prophetic Forecast: Unlocking the Concept

How do keys and destiny connections connect? What needs to be unlocked in us through relationships? Well, God downloaded more revelation to me. Keys can lead us to the right connections, and they can also close the wrong connections. Not only do we have the keys to bind and loose, but we also can open and lock the doors. We can establish boundaries to legislate what has permission to stay and go. Remember keys give us authority. Those who possess the key are authority figures who can decide if someone or something can enter a space.

Sometimes a decision is one of the most powerful keys we can have.

We can also close the door on our past by locking it with our peace. If a relationship no longer brings us peace, its assignment has come to an end. We can release it with a turn of our key that gives us peace and seek the right relationship that we need to unlock the next in our destinies. Not only can we open and close doors when it comes to destiny connections, but we

also need to understand how keys and their locks give insight on the magnitude of these God-ordained relationships. As God kept illuminating revelations about keys, He pointed out something significant about their design.

He said, “If you look at the keys, they are cut a certain way, and they're cut a certain way to fit a certain lock. Most people are trying to fit the wrong key in wrong locks.”

That's even in connections, and that's why nothing has worked for some of us. We have not connected with the right person that those grooves are literally cut out for.

The Lord then began to tell me that a lot of things we think are warfare, they are not. It’s Him saying, “You are at the door, and I've already shown you the future, but you just don't know how to unlock the door.”

And I said, "God, I don't understand this."

He said, "You got to understand what I mean by these keys."

The keys that we hold open more than doors. They unlock partnerships, territories, domains, and jurisdiction.

As I began looking for the meaning, the one person who came to mind was Elisha. He could not continue to work for his family; he needed to go and stay with Elijah until the older prophet could unlock some places where he

needed to go. There are doors where people can't get into because of connections. I tell people who travel with me all the time, "Guess what? You could be called to the nations. But who unlocks the door for you?"

Many believers are standing in front of the right doors, but they have the wrong keys. For example, I could be standing in front of another apostle's door thinking that this apostle was supposed to open the door for me, and God never intended on that person to open the door.

What do you do when God blocks the connection? Submit your heart to Him, surrender what you thought, and rededicate your yes. Wrong keys are costly. They can cause wrong turns that can delay or deter you, or even worse, sabotage your destiny (1 Kings 13:11-24; Judges 15:17-19). They can detour the lives of those who need you to open the door for them.

What would have happened to the Shunammite woman?
What would have happened to the widow woman
with the oil?
What would have happened to Naaman?
What would have happened to them
if Elisha chose to not follow Elijah that day?

Elisha was sitting there plowing for his father and thinking that he was the key, but Elijah was the one who was going to open the door for him.

So many people are still at point A because they're standing in front of the wrong door. It's not that the door is not there. They are waiting for the

wrong person to open the door for them. And so many people stay stuck in seasons that they're not supposed to be in.

God sends specific people into our lives, not to just unlock the door, but to be the key to get us into our destinies. What they carry is a simple key. It's their access or insight into areas that we need to enter. They've walked in those areas, or they've been there, and God is using them as that vehicle to open that up for us.

Prophetic Process: Getting to the Right Key

I tell people on a platform and people who travel with me that the places that are opening up for us, God is giving me this opportunity to open these nations up to them because that's where I'm called. And God began to deal with me. He told me to go to Daniel with Gabriel and Michael. Daniel oversaw the nation of Israel, and that nation had to be opened up. So sometimes we're not even connected to angels so that unlocking can take place, and we're traveling in the nations without having access, just like a passport being able to get in.

God said that the people are not taking Him seriously; they're just going places, and they don't really have the access. So I think that it comes down to a person being stuck and saying, "Hey, what did God tell me to do first?" That one question can identify where we got off track for whatever reasons and course correct to get back on God's schedule.

Every key means something, whether people believe it or not. I've never seen it like this. God is really pushing me by telling me what I need to do. I told my staff that we could be somewhere in the nations every single month. That's just how God is opening up the doors. But I'm so focused on trying to develop the U.S. that I had to redo that again because the person that was my vice chair; she was just a wreck. She tried to really undermine and take the thing for herself. So we had to regroup and do things a little differently, but understanding that it's about connections.

Some people who you're connected with are like a puzzle. The top piece doesn't fit the bottom piece, and the middle piece doesn't fit the top piece. You find the piece that fits you correctly, and then I believe that it will be the piece that will unlock what you need.

Keynote Connection: Barak

Judges 4:9, 22 (NKJV): "So she said, 'I will surely go with you; nevertheless there will be no glory for you in the journey you are taking, for the Lord will sell Sisera into the hand of a woman.' Then Deborah arose and went with Barak to Kedesh. . . And then, as Barak pursued Sisera, Jael came out to meet him, and said to him, 'Come, I will show you the man whom you seek.' And when he went into her tent, there lay Sisera, dead with the peg in his temple."

Barak's story is a great example that further illustrates how destiny connections are like a puzzle, each piece fulfilling its purpose when in the right position. Deborah and Jael symbolized how the prophetic and the practical partnered together to push destiny into action, even when the vessel was hesitant to make the first step.

Deborah was his first destiny connection. At first, one might think that she was the key to the door that would lead to victory over Sisera, but she was not. She used the keys of worship, military strategy, and prophecy to get Barak prepared and in position for victory. Deborah also represented access to the door of deliverance. She helped Barak in dealing with the lower ranks of the enemy. This tactical warfare strategy weakened the infrastructure as they dealt with the foot soldiers.

She also represented the key of a kingdom mindset or mind of Christ. She stood by the word of the Lord and allowed it to determine how she thought about what she experienced. She encouraged Barak to do the same. Deborah prophesied the outcome by exhorting, edifying, and comforting Barak.

Jael uses the key of the practical to open the door of victory for Barak. Hospitality, a warm bowl of milk, and a tent peg were unlikely weaponry that took down Sisera. She also represented inner healing. Our mindsets must shift in order to enter doors of healing and deliverance, prosperity and overflow, and deliverance and breakthrough.

Chapter Forward: Breaking New Ground with the Right Connections

This chapter dealt with the role of relationships and connections in unlocking potential and destiny. Relationships are used to open and close doors, and the past is locked out by our stance of peace. Not every connection is the right one, and the right person is often needed to unlock specific doors in one's life. Wrong connections can keep people stuck in unproductive seasons. The chapter concludes with the analogy of puzzle pieces being used to illustrate that only the correct fit will unlock what is needed. The destiny connections between Elijah and Elisha as well as Barak, Deborah, and Jael help us to understand how keys can build upon each other to birth out destiny. The process of finding the right key or destiny connection can be tough, but one must be willing to rethink the framework of process of timing. It's time for a shift.

CHAPTER 4

Keys as a Framework of Rethinking Process and Timing

1 Kings 19:19-21 (NKJV): "Then he said, 'Go, borrow vessels from everywhere, from all your neighbors—empty vessels; do not gather just a few. And when you have come in, you shall shut the door behind you and your sons; then pour it into all those vessels, and set aside the full ones.'

So she went from him and shut the door behind her and her sons, who brought the vessels to her; and she poured it out. Now it came to pass, when the vessels were full, that she said to her son, 'Bring me another vessel.' And he said to her, 'There is not another vessel.' So the oil ceased. Then she came and told the man of God. And he said, 'Go, sell the oil and pay your debt; and you and your sons live on the rest.'"

Prophetic Forecast: Unlocking the Concept

We have covered much in the past three chapters as we have expanded our understanding of spiritual keys. Our assignments, our mantles, and our destinies are not just about us; they are about the kingdom of God advancing, and they are connected to people.

As apostles, we are not only building systems, businesses, ministries, and movements; we are building and equipping people.

People's lives and destinies are at stake. We must allow vision to guide us as we move forward with keys that give revelation, authority, access, responsibility, stewardship, and destiny connections. We must see how maturity, readiness, process, right doors and keys, destiny connections, and timing are important to navigate wisely.

Even though we know that we need to make sure we have the right key for the right door, we must rethink our approach to the process and divine timing. The process prepares us while the timing develops us. Both teach us to discern the times and seasons and know when to use the keys, while patience completes her perfect work.

Part of the process involves enduring the cuts. Remember the Lord pointed out to me about every key being cut. When a key is made, it is placed inside a machine. There's a loud, grinding noise that fills the air as it is being shaped to fit the right lock. At times, you may even see sparks of light. The process shapes it and prepares it for use.

Apostles have endured cuts as we have pioneered paths forward in our journey. Like a military general who has stripes and bars that signify his or her rank, we have cuts from warfare that not only signify rank, but they also stand as the testimony of evidence that we are built for this. We have to endure them in order to receive the crown.

Jesus underwent the same process during His three-year ministry, and the scriptures say that we must suffer with Him to reign with Him. Jesus is both the door and the key. He is the original pattern of the revelations that have come forth. He went through cuts in His journey on earth to return to His seat of authority, crowned as King of Kings and Lord of Lords.

Everybody wants the crown,
but no one wants the fire
of the process that comes with it.

Rank comes with a price; elevation comes with trials and testing (Mark 10:37-40). Are you really built for this process? Are you really ready to submit to the timing and training of this thing? My God, that is the question right there, emerging pioneer!

Prophetic Framework: All You Have is All You Need

This woman could have let the pressure of the situation get to her. She had debtors making the same type of threats that Jezebel issued out to Elijah. By this time tomorrow, they were coming for her kids to settle her debts. Can you imagine how this woman of God must have felt?

The precious treasure she birthed from her womb had been made equivalent to treasure that cannot escape moth and rust. The pressure was real, the process seemed heightened, and the timing felt accelerated, but she pressed through the weight of the financial yoke and sought the prophet, the one who had the key of counsel in his prophetic mantle and the word of miracles and breakthrough in his mouth.

He asked her a simple question: "What do you have in your house?

Her response led to an unorthodox and unconventional entrepreneurial strategy that transitioned her from the borrower to the lender, from a widow who struggled to a businesswoman who now entered early retirement. She had a mindset to work the overflow.

The widow woman with the oil in 2 Kings 4 gives us the prophetic framework that contains seven (7) keys that reframe the power of process and timing. This practical application led to a prophetic shift in her life.

7 Keys to Reframe Process and Timing into a Prophetic Shift:

1. Follow the Instruction (Key of Obedience)
2. Yield to the Process (Key of Submission)
3. Move in Faith (Key of Right Timing)
4. Shut Out the Distractions (Key of Focus)
5. Pour Out What You Have (Key of Innovation)
6. Work the Plan (Key of Strategy)
7. Pivot to the Pleasant Place (Key of Prosperity)

Keynote Connection: Jacob/Israel

Genesis 32:24-27 (NKJV): "Then Jacob was left alone; and a Man wrestled with him until the breaking of day. Now when He saw that He did not prevail against him, He touched the socket of his hip; and the socket of Jacob's hip was out of joint as He wrestled with him. And He said, 'Let Me go, for the day breaks.' But he said, 'I will not let You go unless You bless me!'"

Jacob was in transition as he was on his way with his family to make amends with his brother Esau. Bitterness and betrayal caused fraternal separation. The loss of a birthright and blessing made them strangers. But the keys of process and timing changed Jacob's name, his life, his identity, and his nature. Before he could fully embrace the path that Israel must take and completely close the door to his past as Jacob, he had to forgive and reconcile.

The key of reconciliation is powerful. It's even a ministry through Jesus Christ that brings us back to God and institutes us as ambassadors of Jesus Christ. It is better to reconcile a covenantal relationship than to dismantle it.

Daybreak was more than the sun brightening up the sky; it was the Son bringing healing in His wings to a generational line.

It takes a process to break things out of us, off of us, and through us. We have to wrestle with our flesh, our trauma, our soul wounds, and familial proclivities to be healthy and whole enough to receive the keys God wants to give us. The keys of process and timing can help us to get to that place through the grace, mercy, and love of Jesus Christ.

Chapter Forward: Breaking New Ground with the Right Strategy

This chapter dealt with a deeper exploration of process and timing and the prophetic revelation about keys being cut. We recognized that the cuts testify to the process and the rank. The cuts can also be seen as pruning so that we can bear fruit that remains. For that is what Jesus was looking for when He saw the fig tree in Mark 11. It was what God was looking for in Luke 13 when Jesus pleaded with Him to give it more time. Fruit bears witness to work being done and making kingdom impact.

The chapter then used the widow woman with oil to present a prophetic framework to guide us on how practical application can cause prophetic shifts in our lives. All we need to do is connect what we have inside of us and our homes with the right strategy.

It ended with Jacob showing us how the keys of process and timing can lead to reconciliation and transformation. Now let's continue to unlock principles of the spiritual keys that can not only liberate our souls, but also relocate us back to financial dominion.

CHAPTER 5

Keys to Deliverance Doors: Reframing Prosperity and Poverty

Psalm 118:24-25 (NKJV): "This is the day the Lord has made; we will rejoice and be glad in it. Save now, I pray, O Lord; O Lord, I pray, send now prosperity.

Prophetic Forecast: Unlocking the Concept

Overcoming obstacles can be overwhelming. Whatever the circumstance may be, a person will continually look for a way of escape. They need a strategy to serve as a key to gain access to the deliverance door, and that key of strategy can be found in the Word of God.

I believe this is what happened in Jericho (Joshua 6). Jericho had to be unlocked by the strategy God gave them. Who could imagine walking around a large wall for six days without saying a word? Who would have thought that praise would set in motion a divine intervention in land conquest? The key of strategy and the key of praise were powerful, unconventional tools.

In Psalm 119:113, the psalmist writes that his steps are ordered in the word and no iniquity can have dominion over him. In Galatians 6:17, Paul proclaims that he bears the marks of Jesus Christ in his body and that no principality can have dominion over him. No principality, no iniquity, no obstacle can have the victory or the rule. So we must search out the scriptures for the strategy to conquer it.

Jesus has already settled it on the Cross.
He is the strongman of our homes, our temples, and our souls.

These obstacles can occur in our faith, our families, or our finances. With finances, we have to look at it from a spiritual perspective. The deliverance door is there as an exit strategy, but there are two spirits that play a part in whether you cross the threshold of that door or not: the spirit of poverty and the spirit of prosperity.

The spirit of poverty is a stronghold within the mind that moves a person out of dominion through a lack mindset. It causes them to remain in a stuck place, always believing that they will never have enough. This is far from the truth. Psalm 24 tells us that the earth is the Lord's and the fullness thereof. He supplies all our need according to His riches and glory, and He is our Redeemer who gives us the power to get wealth (Philippians 4:19; Deuteronomy 8:18).

The spirit of prosperity is one of a kingdom mindset, one that understands how the kingdom economy operates. Those who desire prosperity understand the principles of tithing, sowing, and first fruits. They have a spirit of generosity, and in fact, have used it as a key. In order for people to walk through deliverance doors, they must reframe poverty and prosperity and use truth as the key to unlock those doors.

If somebody's dealing with poverty, they've got to have prosperity unlocked.

Prophetic Revelation: Jesus Unlocks Truth for Supernatural Provision

There are two examples in the Bible that I would like to share. The first one is in Matthew 17:24-27. Here we see Peter has been confronted with not paying the temple tax. He mentions it to Jesus. Jesus states that they were not servants, but sons. He still renders to Caesar what belongs to him, and He tells Peter to look in the mouth of a fish. I believe that there was an unlocking for him to go to be able to find the provision. Some people said it was a miracle, but I believe that God unlocked truth for him to be able to go.

The second example is in Luke 5:4-7. Jesus told the disciples to launch into the deep and go into an area that they had never been before. He told them to cast on a side that they had never cast before. People look at that as a miracle, but I look at it as if he unlocks something that was not available for anybody else.

In both cases, He unlocked the supernatural that was

created just for them. Jesus was a key because the disciples happened to be with him at both moments. He was the connection because of the relationship that he had with them. So when a relationship unlocks prosperity, it closes up poverty. The big key is recognizing which relationships can do what.

If I'm looking for a car, then I've got to find the right car that fits me. You have to find the right key that fits you. This applies to everybody in the Body of Christ. I always give the hamburger analogy. Let's say you love a hamburger with tomatoes, pickles, and the works. You go to Burger King, and they don't fix it the way that you get it at McDonald's. To you, that burger is horrible. But you go to Wendy's and you love it.

So when the apostles and bishops or whoever is ministering to you, you say that they have the keys that fit. That's good. Why? Because they have the key to really lock; it's not a one-time thing. It's a consistent thing.

Christ was always consistent. He may not have done it the same way all the time, but Christ was always consistent. And so the person who has the key to unlock, it's not going to taste bad. You're going to be like alright, that's good. So you won't be saying that you didn't get anything out of that. You won't be asking, "Where were they?" It won't feel like it's hit or miss. It will be good. That's how I test to see if the relationship will stick or not.

Prophetic Strategy: Financial Keys for Legacy Building

One part of legacy building is having life insurance to cover your family, ministry, or business when you die. Depending on how much money you have coming in into your business, from a tax-free perspective, putting all that money in an insurance plan is going to save you way more money than letting it show up for taxes. Investing in life insurance helps you to be on the road to wealth and break the barrier of poverty in your life and in your generational line. It also provides security for leaders and their organizations.

Keynote Connection: Isaac

Genesis 26:12-13 (NKJV): "Then Isaac sowed in that land, and reaped in the same year a hundredfold; and the Lord blessed him. The man began to prosper, and continued prospering until he became very prosperous."

Isaac's story shows us what the key of prosperity looks like in action. He followed the Lord's instruction to stay in a land where there was a famine. There was an opportunity for the spirit of poverty to settle. Isaac could have focused on the lack around him, disobeyed God, and left for Egypt. But he didn't. He sowed in the land and reaped a bountiful harvest. We also see how sowing and reaping are not only supernatural kingdom laws, but they are also the right keys to close the door to poverty functioning through famine.

Isaac also had the key that opened the door of abundance. Each well opened up a flow and brought increase. This increase caused spiritual warfare to arise from a longtime enemy, the Philistines. As Isaac abounded in wealth and land, they fought back by filling his wells with dirt.

Isaac finally found himself at another well and he named it Rehoboth. The name unlocked further prosperity, for it meant that God had made room for him and he would be fruitful in the land. His last well was in Beersheba. This brought forth a sevenfold stream because there were seven wells in total there. The key of obedience led to Isaac walking through the door of generational wealth.

Chapter Forward: Breaking New Ground with the Right Financial Deliverance

This chapter discusses the spiritual principle that keys can unlock prosperity and close the door on poverty. Biblical examples that both involve Peter and Jesus are interpreted as unlocking supernatural provision rather than mere miracles. Through the stories of finding provision in a fish's mouth and casting a net to bring in a greater surplus, we begin to see the supernatural overflow and understand the principle of streams. The key of truth is presented as a powerful tool of deliverance. The chapter revisits the principle of having the right relationships and ends with a legacy-building strategy for generational wealth and a discussion on Isaac.

CHAPTER 6

Questions as Keys for Revelation and Redirection

Esther 4:14 (NKJV): "'For if you remain completely silent at this time, relief and deliverance will arise for the Jews from another place, but you and your father's house will perish. Yet who knows whether you have come to the kingdom for such a time as this?'"

Prophetic Forecast: Unlocking the Concept

Before we unlock the last concept in this book, let's do a brief recap of the power principles we have discovered so far:

- The power of a key to unlock transition, territories, testimonies, and truth.
- The power of a door to unlock access, alignment, mantles, and mandates.
- The power of a prophetic act to unlock miracles, momentum, faith, and fulfillment.
- The power of a kingdom principle to unlock a shift, a stream, a disruption, and a dispensation.

- The power of a question to unlock position, purpose, revelation, and redirection.

Questions are keys that can alert us to where we are and where we need to be. They are an alignment check in the soul and the spirit and a disruption that can shake up comfort zones. They uncover what's been hidden and release what's been locked up.

A question can jumpstart a destiny move and a mindset shift.

Mordecai challenged Esther with a question. Favor had made a way for her to become the queen. Perhaps this favor was for this moment. She had an opportunity to use her voice and position as keys to open the deliverance door for her people. The power of life and death were indeed in her tongue, but this decision posed a risk to her own life and comfortability.

This question required a significant shift for Esther: a young woman who lost her parents at a very young age and succeeded the first queen who lost her life for rebelling a king's order. Her answer depended on what her mind chose to magnify. This question was a multi-level one:

- Should Esther exchange an orphan mindset for a kingdom mindset?
- Should she look out for herself, or should she become a voice for the voiceless?

- Should she remain hidden, or should she be bold enough to be seen?

Her answer became an advocate.

Esther used one of the most powerful keys that we have as believers, the key of prayer and fasting. For Jesus said in Matthew 17, that this kind could only come out by this way. For Esther, this kind was the spirit of pride and the spirit of murder operating through Haman. This kind sought to take out a whole nation over one offense: Mordecai refused to bow.

Fasting and prayer gave Esther the strategy on how to approach the king and secure a divine reversal for the Jews. One question unlocked destiny and dominion for Esther, destruction and death for Haman and his family, and promotion and prosperity for Mordecai.

Questions are kingdom keys of quantum release.

Prophetic Revelation: Questions That Shift

Sometimes questions aren't asked just for answers, but for awareness and assessment. They can be a measuring line or a rod of correction. They may be a signal to move forward, come up higher, or be transparent. They may also unlock what is needed to leave a legacy through the written word.

Questions are apostolic; they build upon what is asked.

Whenever God asks a question, it's usually for revelation and redirection. It is never to secure information because He is all-knowing. Whenever Jesus asked a question, it became a teaching moment, a truth reveal, and a catalyst for healing, deliverance, and change. Each time a question was asked in Scripture, it became a key that shifted a person, a nation, a territory, or a mindset. Questions cultivate wholeness.

Engaging in questions with God helped me to unlock obedience, insight, revelation, miracles, and this book that you hold in your hands. I was willing to ask instead of moving forward in my own intellect. He gave me the visions; I received them, searched out the matter, and followed instructions. I was willing to listen to His questions, being transparent in my answers even if I didn't have one. Sometimes there were no questions, just following the leading of the Holy Spirit.

There is a difference between questions that lead to revelation and redirection and questions that lead to confusion and doubt. As you reflect and commune with the Lord, may your discernment be ever sharper to recognize the difference and allow questions to transition you to the next level. Never underestimate the power of a question.

Keynote Connection: Paul and Silas

Acts 26:25-26 (NKJV): "But at midnight Paul and Silas were praying and singing hymns to God, and the prisoners were listening to them. Suddenly there was a great earthquake, so that the foundations of the prison were shaken; and immediately all the doors were opened, and everyone's chains were loosed."

This story demonstrates the power of three keys: the key of prayer and intercession, the key of praise, and the key of timing. Prayer is a weapon, a worship and communion with God, and a kingdom technology. It draws on the presence and the strength of the Lord because He honors His word. The angels respond to the law of the Lord. The Courts of Heaven respond to the governing power of our decrees (Psalm 119:89-90).

Praise is a power key because it produces a sound that invites God to inhabit and dwell. It magnifies Him above all circumstances and confuses the enemy. The Roman soldiers surrounding Paul and Silas were probably perplexed with their songs of praise. They were chained and fettered, beaten and mistreated, and had the nerve to exalt the Lord despite it all.

The Roman soldiers learned that doors didn't always need a physical key to open them; the voiceprint of the believer who understood his authority could shatter that door and release a ripple effect throughout the earth. We must never lose our praise, no matter what.

Finally, midnight is important because it is the third prayer watch. This is the time to war for spiritual protection against witchcraft. It is the time to fight for deliverance and breakthrough. Again, timing is an important key.

Midnight signals the transition from one day to a new one. The former can no longer speak into the present. What was bound must be set free. A threefold key unlocked a threefold deliverance that brought forth salvation to a Roman soldier and his family.

No matter the key, may each one lift up Christ glorified.

Bonus Keynote Connection: Jesus Christ

Matthew 26:40-41 (NKJV): "Then He came to the disciples and found them sleeping, and said to Peter, 'What! Could you not watch with Me one hour? Watch and pray, lest you enter into temptation. The spirit indeed is willing, but the flesh is weak.'"

The question was a rebuke to realign. Jesus was at one of His weakest moments where He was struggling with His will. This moment of transparency and vulnerability needed to be covered in prayer and intercession. But His disciples fell asleep and could not keep the watch.

After the question, Jesus gave the principle. The fact that this happened three times confirmed His admonishment about the flesh being weak. This question was a key that opened up invitation and intimacy. It established the pattern of devotional time. What did it look like to be in the secret place? Peter, James, and John had front-row seats to the answer, but they were unable to stay awake to receive the impartation.

Apostolic builders and forerunners must have a prayer life. We must guard the vision with strategic intercession and spiritual intelligence. We must follow Jesus Christ as our main example. He is the paradigm of breaking new ground. For even He was crucified so salvation and redemption could come forth (John 12:24). He broke new ground by tearing the veil of separation between mankind and God.

He is the key to note and connect to as apostles build visions and people while serving as keys that equip the ecclesia.

Vision Forward: Breaking New Ground with the Right Questions

This chapter began with a brief recap of what the power of a key, door, kingdom principle, and question can accomplish. Through Esther's story, she had one question that pushed her into action and prompted a destiny move. The chapter then explained how questions were used in the Bible, but the common thread throughout the chapter was the key of prayer intercession. In both keynote connections, this key brought breakthrough and gave insight on how to use it to guard our visions.

As this book comes to an end, may your vision continue to move forward as you break new ground. Be willing to allow the right questions to guide you in the right direction.

ABOUT THE AUTHOR

Archbishop Dr. Mitchell L. Foster, Sr. was born in Cocoa, Florida. He is the third of three children born to Lee and Betty Foster. At a young age, Archbishop Dr Mitchell. Foster began to feel that God had a particular calling on his life to feed, teach, and nurture as well as equipping and activating souls for the kingdom.

He responded to the call by preaching his initial sermon at *Reaching Out to Help You Christian Center, Inc.* in Baltimore, Maryland, under the leadership of Apostle Dr. Michael Foster. In 1970, Bishop Dr. Foster was ordained by laying on of the hands by Apostle James Parson, Sr. of the *True Fellowship Interdenominational Ministry,* and later affirmed as an Apostle by Apostle Dr Moran Lowe. As God continued to elevate Bishop Dr. Mitchell Foster to a new level, he was consecrated to the office of Bishop in 2009 under the fellowship of *GRWI* under the leadership of Apostle R. L. Vinson. Bishop Dr. Mitchell Foster has been doing Apostolic work over the years by establishing churches in Africa, Europe, Mexico, Spain, Germany, U.S., Canada, Jamaica, and the United Kingdom. On June 4, 2022, Bishop Dr. Mitchell L Foster was Elevated to Office of Archbishop by Archbishop Dr. Frederick T. Nah, Jr.

Under Archbishop Dr Mitchell Foster's leadership, the church began a community outreach program, which partnered with *Baltimore City Police Department of the Southwest District*, as well as collaborated with the *Antioch Homeless Shelter*, where Archbishop Dr. Mitchell Foster helped with mentoring and counseling in the shelter's men's program. He continued to develop several other outreach programs at *Reaching Out to Help You Christian Center, Inc.*, such as a prison ministry, nursing home ministry, and men's substance abuse Bible study. Dr. Foster led by example and served his congregation, as Christ did His disciples.

Archbishop Dr. Mitchell Foster received his bachelor's in theology from the *Family Bible Seminary*; based in Baltimore, Maryland in 2001. God led Archbishop Dr. Foster on a two-year sabbatical in 2003, where he stepped down as pastor of *Reaching Out to Help You Christian Center, Inc.* and moved to Vero Beach, Florida. While in Florida, the Holy Spirit used Archbishop Dr. Foster to minister through radio broadcast and marriage enrichment seminars.

In 2005, Archbishop Dr. Mitchell Foster became the Senior Pastor of *Tried Stone Church in Middletown*, Ohio. As Pastor of *Tried Stone Church*, Archbishop Dr. Mitchell Foster has developed a mentoring program for at-risk youths and provided transportation service to get them back to school. Archbishop, along with his wife, set up two daycares and houses for women and men to move into after living in the shelter. They also set up seven transitional homes as well as a transportation service for youth getting to school.

Archbishop also developed the *Fresh Touch School of Learning Bible College*. He serves on the Board of Directors as Executive Director of two homeless shelters, *Hope House Rescue Mission* and the *Center for Women and Children.* In August 2016, Archbishop Dr. Foster stepped down as Pastor of Tried Stone. God led him to plant a new church in Dayton Ohio.

Archbishop Dr. Foster also served on the faith-based community board for *Warren County Correctional Institution and the Middletown Historical Society*. Archbishop Dr. Mitchell Foster also had served as the President of the *Union Fellowship of Middletown* and was selected by the *NAACP Middletown* branch to serve as the 1st Vice-President of its religious committee. In 2007, Dr. Foster received his Doctorate in Philosophy and Theology from the *Believers University* and is currently working on his *Doctorate degree in Clinical Counseling and Temperament Theory.* In Feb. of 2008, Archbishop Dr. Foster was instrumental in starting the first *African American Museum* in Middletown, Ohio. In January 2023, Archbishop had written his first book called *Getting out of the Boat.*

Archbishop Dr. Foster is also involved in international missions' work. He travels to Kingston, Jamaica annually as well as Ghana, Nigeria, Canada, London, Zimbabwe, Spain, Grenada, Cayman Islands, and Nassau, Bahamas. Archbishop Dr. Mitchell Foster works with newly installed Bishops, Apostles, Pastors, and Prophets with leadership development and church growth. He has been on the *Word Network* sometimes with his spiritual mother Dr Taketa Williams on the Shift Program.

Archbishop Dr. Mitchell Foster is married to Terrie O. Foster. They are the parents of five children: Leondra, Keondra, Courtnie, Ashleigh, and Mitchell, Jr. as well as three grandchildren.

www.ingramcontent.com/pod-product-compliance
Lightning Source LLC
LaVergne TN
LVHW011051110826
845149LV00015B/3449
* 9 7 9 8 9 9 0 1 3 0 2 5 8 *